DK READERS is a compelling program for beginning readers, designed in conjunction with leading literacy experts, including Dr. Linda Gambrell, distinguished Professor of Education at Clemson University. Dr. Gambrell has served as President of the National Reading Conference, the College Reading Association, and the International Reading Association.

Beautiful illustrations and superb full-color photographs combine with engaging, easy-to-read stories to offer a fresh approach to each subject in the series. Each DK READER is guaranteed to capture a child's interest while developing his or her reading skills, general knowledge, and love of reading.

The five levels of DK READERS are aimed at different reading abilities, enabling you to choose the books that are exactly right for your child:

DISCARD

Pre-level 1: Learning to read
Level 1: Beginning to read
Level 2: Beginning to read alone
Level 3: Reading alone
Level 4: Proficient readers

The "normal" age at which a child begins to read can be anywhere from three to eight years old. Adult participation through the lower levels is very helpful for providing encouragement, discussing storylines, and sounding out unfamiliar words.

No matter which level you select, you can be sure that you are helping your child learn to read, then read to learn!

LONDON, NEW YORK, MUNICH,
MELBOURNE, and DELHI

Author Laura Buller
Senior Editor Cécile Landau
Senior Art Editor Ann Cannings
Senior DTP Designer David McDonald
Senior Producer Pieta Pemberton
Associate Publisher Nigel Duffield

Reading Consultant
Deborah Lock

First American Edition, 2013

Published in the United States by DK Publishing
375 Hudson Street, New York, New York 10014

001–192463–Jul/13

Copyright © 2013 Dorling Kindersley Limited

DK books are available at special discounts when purchased in bulk
for sales promotions, premiums, fund-raising, or educational use.
For details, contact:
DK Publishing Special Markets
375 Hudson Street
New York, New York 10014
SpecialSales@dk.com

A catalog record for this book is available
from the Library of Congress.

ISBN: 978-1-4654-0951-5

Printed and bound in China by
L. Rex Printing Co. Ltd.

The publisher would like to thank the following for their kind
permission to reproduce their photographs:
Alamy Images: Blickwinkel 20-21; Myrleen Pearson 11; Suretha
Rous 26-27. **Corbis**: image100 33; Michael Christopher Brown /
National Geographic Society 30-31; Ocean 16-17; Peter Frank 4-5,
8-9, 22, 24-25; Waltraud Grubitzsch / DPA 28-29. **FLPA**: Chris and
Tilde Stuart 14-15, 23. **Getty Images**: Digital Vision / Thomas
Northcut 10-11; Meg Takamura 12-13.

Jacket images: Front: **Getty Images**: Aurora / David McLain.

All other images © Dorling Kindersley
For further information see: www.dkimages.com

Discover more at
www.dk.com

Contents

DK READERS

BEGINNING TO READ ALONE

2

Tracking

Written by Laura Buller

DK

DK Publishing

Be Prepared

Three boys gathered at the edge of the woods, chattering excitedly. They double-checked their gear: spotter's guides, magnifying glasses, notebooks, and phones. Nate, Aaron, and Sam were getting ready to find out which animals made their homes here. They weren't looking for animals, though. Instead, they were hunting for signs the animals left behind.

"This is a good place to search," said Nate. "There's a stream for animals to drink from, and lots of things to eat."

"There are plenty of places to hide and shelter, too!" added Sam. "Let's go."

First Steps

Not long after the boys stepped into the shady woods, Aaron spotted something. A fork-shaped animal track in the soft, muddy ground at the edge of the trail caught his eye. "Check it out, guys!" he cried.

"Cool! Remember what we learned in Scouts about fork-shaped tracks?" said Sam. "They're almost always made by birds," the others exclaimed.

"What kind of bird do you think took a little hike right here?" asked Aaron.

Nate flipped through the pages in his spotter's guide. "Well, if it's a bird that lives on the ground most of the time, its tracks will be one after another."

"Just like us!" Sam grinned. "Aaron, do you see any more tracks down there?"

Aaron studied the ground for clues. Next to the first track, he noticed a fainter one. Then, he found another pair of tracks a couple of inches away.

"Hey, look...the tracks are in pairs," said Aaron.

Sam thought for a moment. "That probably means they belong to a bird that spends a lot of time perching up in the trees. The tracks are in pairs because it hops along the ground."

"They are kind of small.
I almost didn't notice them,"
said Aaron. "My guess would be
they belong to a sparrow."

Aaron snapped a picture with
his camera phone, while the boys
took a note of their findings.
Sam wandered a
little way ahead,
then he stopped
suddenly in
his tracks.

Counting Toes

"Check out these paw-shaped tracks!" Sam said, waving his friends over to a muddy patch, close to a fence near the stream. "There are so many."

Aaron and Nate caught up with their friend. "I remember what to do next," said Nate. "Count the toes."

"I have ten," Sam joked.

Nate rolled his eyes. "Not you, Sam. The toes on the tracks!"

Sam leaned down with his magnifying glass. "There are definitely four, maybe five.

Aaron knelt down to take a closer look. "OK, the tracks are definitely longer than my little finger, more than an inch for sure, so the critter who left them behind can't be too small."

"Unless it has big feet like yours," Sam teased his friend.

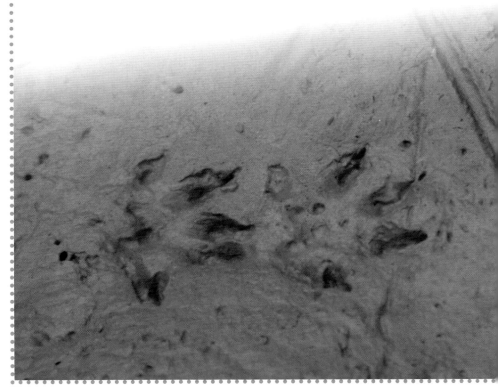

Nate flipped through the spotter's guide. "Hey, does it look like these prints are made by both front and back paws? Are there four toe prints in the front and five at the back?" he quizzed his friends.

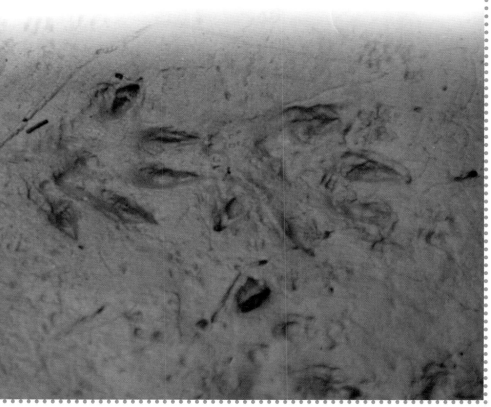

Aaron climbed up onto the fence and looked down to examine the marks more closely. It was hard to make everything out in the damp earth, but he began to notice a pattern.

"I'm almost certain the animals who passed by here had five toes at the front and five at the back." Aaron reported to his friends.

"Those tracks might belong to a family of moles," said Nate. "The size is about right, and there will be plenty of earthworms in the muddy soil. You know worms are a mole's favorite snack. Mmmmm!"

Making Tracks

The boys snapped a few photos and moved on. Sunlight barely reached this part of the woods. Nate looked around, wondering if any animals were watching them...big animals! Lost in thought, he didn't notice large paw-shaped tracks in the trail.

He nearly walked right over them, but Sam threw out his arm to stop his friend.

"Hey, dude, you just about tracked over a track," Sam laughed. "Now what have we here?"

Sam studied the tracks.
It was hard to see in the dim
light, but he could just make
out some toe prints.

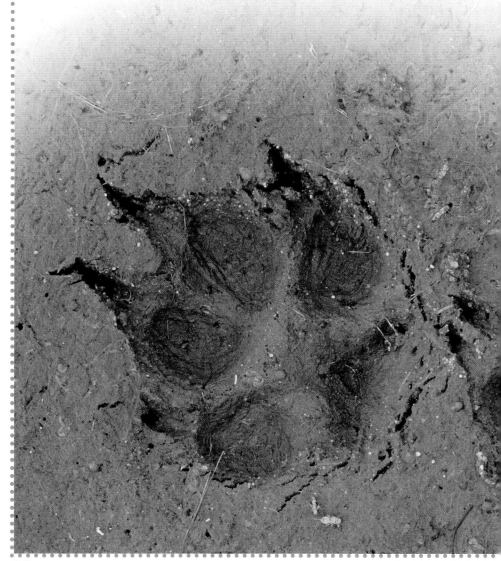

Aaron used his phone to shine a beam of light on the guidebook. "OK, the guide says four front toes and four back toes might belong to some kind of dog or cat. If there is one more toe at the back, we could be looking at a squirrel track. What do you see, bud?"

Nate squinted his eyes to help him focus. "I can't really see," he said.

"That might mean you've tracked a rabbit, or a deer." said Aaron. "Their tracks are not very deep."

"No, hang on, here's a really clear one. One, two, three, four, five...five toes front and back. It's a skunk!" Sam shouted as a strong smell made his nostrils tingle. "Let's make tracks!"

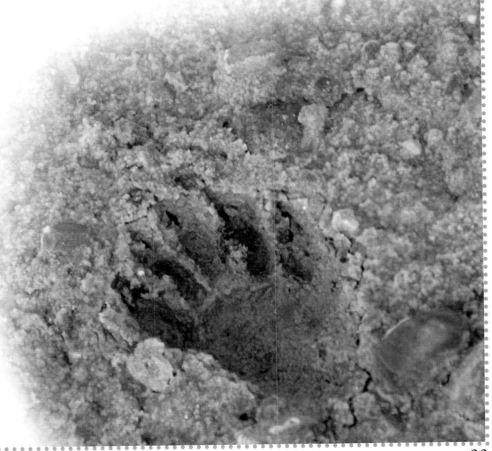

Spotting More Signs

The boys made a quick move, and soon they reached a grassy clearing ringed with trees. "How are we going to see anything if we can't see the ground?" Sam grumbled.

"There are lots of clues to look for!" Aaron replied. "Take a look at these branches. Some hungry animal has had a little nibble recently, maybe a rabbit. You can track animals by the marks they make chewing or biting things."

Nate pointed out some marks on a tree trunk. "These could have been made by a deer rubbing its antlers."

The boys continued across the clearing. They had nearly come full circle, back to where they started.

"Another way to track a creature is spotting all the things animals build, like mole tunnels, chipmunk burrows-even bird's nests or beaver's dams." Nate added. Aaron thought about all the other things animals leave behind. Then he very nearly stepped in some!

"Whoops!" Aaron said as he hopped over a pile of animal scat. "An animal has definitely been here. And gone here."

The boys shared a giggle. "Experienced nature spotters can identify different types of scat and say just what kind of animal made it," said Sam.

"That's gross, but kind of cool!" Aaron said. "Still, I'm glad I didn't put my foot in it."

Suddenly, Nate stopped laughing. He was very quiet and was staring down at the ground. What had he seen?

Trick or Treat!

Nate was deadly quiet.

"What is it?" Sam whispered, more than a little scared.

"It's a big one, all right. A real monster. Massive. At least a size twelve." Nate hissed. The boys crowded near to Nate to take a look. "And it looks like he stepped in some chewing gum recently."

Nate's face broke into a grin. He pointed down to Aaron's shoe print, left at the start of their hike. "It's an Aaron."

Laughing, the boys high-fived with Nate.

"You tricked the trackers!" Sam said. He opened his backpack and reached for some trail mix. "That deserves a treat. Let's go home."

Glossary

Antlers
A deer's long horns

Beaver
A small, brown animal with large front teeth, which lives near water

Certain
To feel sure about something

Clearing
An area of land where trees have been removed

Dim
Not very bright or sunny

Exclaim
To cry or shout, often in surprise

Experienced
To have past knowledge or information about something

Fainter
Less clear; weaker

Focus
To see clearly or to concentrate

Grumble
To moan or complain

Hike
To take a long walk in the countryside

Identify
To recognize

Mole
A small animal that digs tunnels and lives underground

Pair
A group of two people or things

Pattern
A set of shapes or markings

Perch
A high place where a bird sits, such as a branch

Scat
Animal droppings

Shelter
To cover or protect

Sparrow
A small, brown-gray bird

Stream
A small river

Tingle
To tickle or sting

9